Emerging Prophets

Discovering Your Metron

Keith B. Ferrante

Emerging Prophets: Discovering Your Metron

This book or parts thereof may not be reproduced in any form, stored in a retrieval system, or transmitted in any form by any means electronic, mechanical, photocopy, recording, or otherwise without prior written permission of the publisher, except as provided by United States of America copyright law.

Published by:
Keith B. Ferrante
6391 Leisure Town Rd.
Vacaville, CA 95687

Ferrante, Keith B. (2016-09-25).
Emerging Prophets Discovering Your Metron

Cover Designer: Heather Ferrante

ISBN-10: 1537646346
ISBN-13: 978-1537646343

Copyright © 2016 Keith Ferrante
All rights reserved.

DEDICATION

This workbook is dedicated to all the unknown prophets out there that do not know how amazing they are and how desperately they are needed in their places of influence!

ACKNOWLEDGMENTS

Thank you so much to my wife Heather for standing by me and helping me birth this prophetic ministry!

Thank you Dan McCollam for being someone who championed me to step into developing prophets. Without your strategies and friendship this workbook would not have resulted.

Thank you so much Tom Parsons for your work on making this workbook look excellent. I'm always amazed at how well you do so many things behind the scenes.

CONTENTS

	Acknowledgments	iv
	Introduction	1
1	Discovering The Places You Are Called To Influence	4
2	Discovering The Leaders You Are Called To Influence	36
3	Discovering The Realms Of Society You Are Called To Influence	60
4	Discovering The People Groups You Are Called To Influence	83
5	Discovering The Issues You Are Called To Deal With	105
6	Discovering The Kingdom Leaders You Are Called To	127
	Final Assessment	149

INTRODUCTION

In this workbook you will go on a journey to discover where and who you are called to serve. This is what we call your platform; the place you release the Kingdom from, your place of influence. So many people think that if they could preach a sermon on Sunday morning in their favorite church then they will finally have arrived at the place of success. Many of the prophets of the Bible never preached one sermon, yet they impacted the world and brought the Kingdom of God wherever they went. Elisha never preached a sermon, Daniel didn't, Joseph, or David, and neither did Esther. But we would consider them heroes of the faith. They are prophets and people that impacted their generation and are still speaking today. This book is here to help you discover where and who you are called to impact. What does your "Platform" look like? 1 Corinthians 12:5 says, "There are different kinds of service, but the same Lord." We all are called to serve somewhere to someone but everyone of us is unique. We each have a different kind of area we are called to serve in, but we all have the same Holy Spirit leading us.

The struggle we've had for so long is that many people don't feel they could possibly be a prophet because they don't look like other prophets or have the same passions or places of influence other prophets have. I want to help us eliminate that error and realize just like Paul and Peter in Galatians 2:8, "For God, who was at work in the ministry of Peter as an apostle to the Jews, was also at work in my ministry as an apostle to the Gentiles." No two persons' arena of influence is alike. Paul was an apostle to the Gentiles and Peter to the Jews. Both were valid apostles with different arenas of influence. In the same way, no two prophets are alike. No one prophet has the same calling as another prophet. There are close to 80 named prophets in the Bible all with different purposes, journeys, skill sets, and callings. My goal in putting together this workbook is to help you go on a journey of discovery that will end with you having much more clarity about where and who you are called to minister to as a prophet.

Discovering Your Metron as an Emerging Prophet

How to use this workbook:

Write in this workbook five of seven days a week for three months. You pick when. At the end of the three months you will put your results on a final results page that will help you identify where and who you are called to serve. Some of these discoveries must be flushed out further to determine if this will become a part of your life calling, but this workbook will get you started on that journey and help you begin to ask the right questions which will lead you to the needed discoveries of who and where you are called to serve.

Many blessings on your journey!

Keith Ferrante

Section 1
Discovering The Places You Are Called to Influence

Section 1: Location Discovery

1. Discovering the specific places, cities, towns, and nations of your heart that you're called to influence.

Years ago I learned that if I wanted to reach every nation in the world I would have to get a heart for every nation in the world. So every morning when I woke up I took a walk. As I saw the sun come over the horizon God would tell me the name of a nation to pray for. I'd pray and prophesy over that nation before I studied up on it. After I had prophesied a while and written down what I saw, then I got online and studied up on the nation. I looked for strengths, weaknesses, struggles, type of government, type of economy, challenges they're facing, and breakthroughs. I looked up the faces of the people in the country, listened to their music styles, and got to know the general heart of that nation. Then I prayed again with the knowledge I had acquired and I would prophesy again with the knowledge I now had. I then built a prayer for that country and a prophetic word for that country and started a journal. Sometimes by the end of that several hour journey, my heart had been so captured by that country that I was weeping and falling in love with the people I had yet to meet. Once on the very day I was praying for a specific country and had fallen in love with that country, God opened up the door through social media for a person from that country to contact me and invite me to come to their country. I knew that getting his heart for a country, city, place or a people group was a key to being given influence there. I may not have gone to every country in the world yet but when I get a chance to meet a person from that country, I already have a bit of God's heart for them because I have already prayed for them. It gives me an edge as a prophetic voice. It is a key to the start of influencing nations.

I have learned to use this skill to get God's heart for cities, regions, states, nations, people groups, churches, and influencers. In this 10-day discovery we are going to help you get started towards discovering the places you have a heart for. We will spend 10 days praying and journaling what we discover. The places you have a bigger heart for will be revealing things you want to remember. Those are telling you places God may have called you to explore at a deeper level. Proverbs 16:9 says, "In his heart a man plans his course, but the Lord determines his steps." When through prayer we begin to discover what is in our hearts for certain locations and people groups, then God will give us the next step to begin to explore further if that is a place we are called to serve in the next season. It doesn't mean we have to move there, although we may, it just means we get to go on a discovery of finding out if that place is an assignment from God for us to explore.

For the first few days we will pray over nations then after that we will move to cities and regions. This is a review of what we are looking to pray over.

Discovering Your Metron as an Emerging Prophet

1. Prophesy over a nation without any further knowledge of that nation's story.

2. Now after you've done that, study up on that nation. What are their strengths, weaknesses, financial situation, history, culture, government style, struggles, inventions, influence, prayer points, and influencers that have come out of that country?

3. Look at the pictures and faces of the people. After that look at the landscape of that country.

4 Listen to the music, look at the art, discover a bit of the culture of that country.

5. Now build a prayer from what you have discovered about that country.

6. Work at it until that country has been embedded into your heart. Some countries you will discover find their way easily into your heart and others are more work. The ones that seem to stay in your heart may be a sign of a group of people that you have a calling to minister to. That is the whole goal of this exercise. To get God's heart for the world but then to find a specific people group God has called you to be a prophet to. Those people could be in your city or in your region or they could be in another part of the world. The key for you is to find out who God has assigned you as an influence to and then to begin to be intentional about engaging them at a strategic level. This is a way to that discovery.

Discovering Your Metron as an Emerging Prophet

Day 1: Nation discovery

1. Pick any nation of the world to pray for. What is the nation called? What did the Lord show you as you started praying and prophesying over that nation?

2. Now study up on that nation. What did the Lord show you after you've done your study up on that nation? What is that nation's strengths, weaknesses, financial situation, history, government style, culture, struggles, inventions, influence, prayer points, and influencers that have come out of that country?

3. Look at the pictures and faces of the people. Look next at the landscape of that country. Did anything begin to happen to your heart in looking at these pictures? What emotions came up?

4. Listen to the music, look at the art, discover a bit of the culture of that country. Did anything happen to your heart in this discovery? What emotions came up?

5. Now build a prayer from what you have discovered about that country. For example, *I pray for America, the land of the free and the home of the brave. You are a beautiful nation of vast diversity. You have seen many challenges but have overcome them well. You have been given much influence. I pray that you would have wisdom to use that influence in a godly way. Father I ask that you would bring a revival in America. Bring her back to her godly roots. Break her free of impurity. Raise up a righteous standard in her. Let an outpouring of the spirit of God flow over you. Open up again the wells of revival that are in your borders. Bring the nation back to God.* There are so many ways to pray for a nation but the main goal is to pray in such a way that your heart starts coming alive for that nation.

6. Finally, how deep did this country get into your heart during this exercise? Between 1 to 5, five being you so fell in love with this nation and one being I did the exercise but I didn't feel much heart connect for that nation. Write your number here and why you wrote that.

Discovering Your Metron as an Emerging Prophet

Day 2: Nation discovery

1. Pick a nation of the world in Africa to pray for. What is the nation called? What did the Lord show you as you started praying and prophesying over that nation?

2. Now study up on that nation. What did the Lord show you after you've done your study up on that nation? What is that nation's strengths, weaknesses, financial situation, history, government style, culture, struggles, inventions, influence, prayer points, and influencers that have come out of that country?

3. Look at the pictures and faces of the people. Look next at the landscape of that country. Did anything begin to happen to your heart in looking at these pictures? What emotions came up?

4. Listen to the music, look at the art, discover a bit of the culture of that country. Did anything happen to your heart in this discovery? What emotions came up?

Discovering Your Metron as an Emerging Prophet

5. Now build a prayer from what you have discovered about that country. For example, *I pray for America, the land of the free and the home of the brave. You are a beautiful nation of vast diversity. You have seen many challenges but have overcome them well. You have been given much influence. I pray that you would have wisdom to use that influence in a godly way. Father I ask that you would bring a revival in America. Bring her back to her godly roots. Break her free of impurity. Raise up a righteous standard in her. Let an outpouring of the spirit of God flow over you. Open up again the wells of revival that are in your borders. Bring the nation back to God.* There are so many ways to pray for a nation but the main goal is to pray in such a way that your heart starts coming alive for that nation.

6. Finally, how deep did this country get into your heart during this exercise? Between 1 to 5, five being you so fell in love with this nation and one being I did the exercise but I didn't feel much heart connect for that nation. Write your number here and why you wrote that.

Day 3: Nation discovery

1. Pick a nation of the world in Asia to pray for. What is the nation called? What did the Lord show you as you started praying and prophesying over that nation?

2. Now study up on that nation. What did the Lord show you after you've done your study up on that nation? What is that nation's strengths, weaknesses, financial situation, history, government style, culture, struggles, inventions, influence, prayer points, and influencers that have come out of that country?

3. Look at the pictures and faces of the people. Look next at the landscape of that country. Did anything begin to happen to your heart in looking at these pictures? What emotions came up?

4. Listen to the music, look at the art, discover a bit of the culture of that country. Did anything happen to your heart in this discovery? What emotions came up?

Discovering Your Metron as an Emerging Prophet

5. Now build a prayer from what you have discovered about that country. For example, *I pray for America, the land of the free and the home of the brave. You are a beautiful nation of vast diversity. You have seen many challenges but have overcome them well. You have been given much influence. I pray that you would have wisdom to use that influence in a godly way. Father I ask that you would bring a revival in America. Bring her back to her godly roots. Break her free of impurity. Raise up a righteous standard in her. Let an outpouring of the spirit of God flow over you. Open up again the wells of revival that are in your borders. Bring the nation back to God.* There are so many ways to pray for a nation but the main goal is to pray in such a way that your heart starts coming alive for that nation.

6. Finally, how deep did this country get into your heart during this exercise? Between 1 to 5, five being you so fell in love with this nation and one being I did the exercise but I didn't feel much heart connect for that nation. Write your number here and why you wrote that.

Discovering Your Metron as an Emerging Prophet

Day 4: Nation discovery

1. Pick a nation of the world in Europe to pray for. What is the nation called? What did the Lord show you as you started praying and prophesying over that nation?

2. Now study up on that nation. What did the Lord show you after you've done your study up on that nation? What is that nation's strengths, weaknesses, financial situation, history, government style, culture, struggles, inventions, influence, prayer points, and influencers that have come out of that country?

3. Look at the pictures and faces of the people. Look next at the landscape of that country. Did anything begin to happen to your heart in looking at these pictures? What emotions came up?

4. Listen to the music, look at the art, discover a bit of the culture of that country. Did anything happen to your heart in this discovery? What emotions came up?

5. Now build a prayer from what you have discovered about that country. For example, *I pray for America, the land of the free and the home of the brave. You are a beautiful nation of vast diversity. You have seen many challenges but have overcome them well. You have been given much influence. I pray that you would have wisdom to use that influence in a godly way. Father I ask that you would bring a revival in America. Bring her back to her godly roots. Break her free of impurity. Raise up a righteous standard in her. Let an outpouring of the spirit of God flow over you. Open up again the wells of revival that are in your borders. Bring the nation back to God.* There are so many ways to pray for a nation but the main goal is to pray in such a way that your heart starts coming alive for that nation.

6. Finally, how deep did this country get into your heart during this exercise? Between 1 to 5, five being you so fell in love with this nation and one being I did the exercise but I didn't feel much heart connect for that nation. Write your number here and why you wrote that.

Day 5: Nation discovery

1. Pick a nation from North or South America to pray for. What is the nation called? What did the Lord show you as you started praying and prophesying over that nation?

2. Now study up on that nation. What did the Lord show you after you've done your study up on that nation? What is that nation's strengths, weaknesses, financial situation, history, government style, culture, struggles, inventions, influence, prayer points, and influencers that have come out of that country?

3. Look at the pictures and faces of the people. Look next at the landscape of that country. Did anything begin to happen to your heart in looking at these pictures? What emotions came up?

4. Listen to the music, look at the art, discover a bit of the culture of that country. Did anything happen to your heart in this discovery? What emotions came up?

5. Now build a prayer from what you have discovered about that country. For example, *I pray for America, the land of the free and the home of the brave. You are a beautiful nation of vast diversity. You have seen many challenges but have overcome them well. You have been given much influence. I pray that you would have wisdom to use that influence in a godly way. Father I ask that you would bring a revival in America. Bring her back to her godly roots. Break her free of impurity. Raise up a righteous standard in her. Let an outpouring of the spirit of God flow over you. Open up again the wells of revival that are in your borders. Bring the nation back to God.* There are so many ways to pray for a nation but the main goal is to pray in such a way that your heart starts coming alive for that nation.

6. Finally, how deep did this country get into your heart during this exercise? Between 1 to 5, five being you so fell in love with this nation and one being I did the exercise but I didn't feel much heart connect for that nation. Write your number here and why you wrote that.

Day 6: Nation discovery

1. Pick a nation from Australia/New Zealand or the island nations (Oceania) to pray for. What is the nation called? What did the Lord show you as you started praying and prophesying over that nation?

2. Now study up on that nation. What did the Lord show you after you've done your study up on that nation? What is that nation's strengths, weaknesses, financial situation, history, government style, culture, struggles, inventions, influence, prayer points, and influencers that have come out of that country?

3. Look at the pictures and faces of the people. Look next at the landscape of that country. Did anything begin to happen to your heart in looking at these pictures? What emotions came up?

4. Listen to the music, look at the art, discover a bit of the culture of that country. Did anything happen to your heart in this discovery? What emotions came up?

5. Now build a prayer from what you have discovered about that country. For example, *I pray for America, the land of the free and the home of the brave. You are a beautiful nation of vast diversity. You have seen many challenges but have overcome them well. You have been given much influence. I pray that you would have wisdom to use that influence in a godly way. Father I ask that you would bring a revival in America. Bring her back to her godly roots. Break her free of impurity. Raise up a righteous standard in her. Let an outpouring of the spirit of God flow over you. Open up again the wells of revival that are in your borders. Bring the nation back to God.* There are so many ways to pray for a nation but the main goal is to pray in such a way that your heart starts coming alive for that nation.

6. Finally, how deep did this country get into your heart during this exercise? Between 1 to 5, five being you so fell in love with this nation and one being I did the exercise but I didn't feel much heart connect for that nation. Write your number here and why you wrote that.

Day 7: Nation discovery

1. Pray for your own country. What is your nation called? What did the Lord show you as you started praying and prophesying over your nation?

2. Now study up on that nation. What did the Lord show you after you've done your study up on that nation? What is that nation's strengths, weaknesses, financial situation, history, government style, culture, struggles, inventions, influence, prayer points, and influencers that have come out of that country?

3. Look at the pictures and faces of the people. Look next at the landscape of that country. Did anything begin to happen to your heart in looking at these pictures? What emotions came up?

4. Listen to the music, look at the art, discover a bit of the culture of that country. Did anything happen to your heart in this discovery? What emotions came up?

5. Now build a prayer from what you have discovered about your country. For example, my country is America, the land of the free and the home of the brave. *You are a beautiful nation of vast diversity. You have seen many challenges but have overcome them well. You have been given much influence. I pray that you would have wisdom to use that influence in a godly way. Father I ask that you would bring a revival in America. Bring her back to her godly roots. Break her free of impurity. Raise up a righteous standard in her. Let an outpouring of the spirit of God flow over you. Open up again the wells of revival that are in your borders. Bring the nation back to God.* There are so many ways to pray for a nation but the main goal is to pray in such a way that your heart starts coming alive for that nation.

6. Finally, how deep did your country get into your heart during this exercise? Between 1 to 5, five being you so fell in love with this nation and one being I did the exercise but I didn't feel much heart connect for that nation. Write your number here and why you wrote that.

Day 8: Regional Discovery

1. Pray for your own state, region, or part of your country. Study up on your state or region. What is that region or state called? What did the Lord show you as you started praying and prophesying over your region?

2. Now study up on that region. What did the Lord show you after you've done your study up on that region? What is that region's strengths, weaknesses, financial situation, history, government style, culture, struggles, inventions, influence, prayer points, and influencers that have come out of that region?

3. Look at the pictures and faces of the people. Look next at the landscape of that region. Did anything begin to happen to your heart in looking at these pictures? What emotions came up?

4. Listen to the music, look at the art, discover a bit of the culture of that state or region. Did anything happen to your heart in this discovery? What emotions came up?

5. Now build a prayer from what you have discovered about your region or state. For example, my state is California, *the land where people came to find gold, where revivals that have shaken nations have been, where the whole world has been influenced good and bad through this state. I pray Father that this state would become known as the state of purity, glory, worship, creativity, and revival that honors Jesus.* There are so many ways to pray for a state or region but the main goal is to pray in such a way that your heart starts coming alive for that place.

6. Finally, how deep did your state or region get into your heart during this exercise? Between 1 to 5, five being you so fell in love with this state/region and one being I did the exercise but I didn't feel much heart connect for that place. Write your number here and why you wrote that.

Day 9: City Discovery

1. Pray for your own city. Study up on your city. What is your city called? What did the Lord show you as you started praying and prophesying over your city?

2. Now study up on your city. What did the Lord show you after you've done your study up on your city? What is your city's strengths, weaknesses, financial situation, history, government style, culture, struggles, inventions, influence, prayer points, and influencers that have come out of your city?

3. Look at the pictures and faces of the people. Look next at the landscape of your city. Did anything begin to happen to your heart in looking at these pictures? What emotions came up?

4. Listen to the music, look at the art, discover a bit of the culture of that city Did anything happen to your heart in this discovery? What emotions came up?

5. Now build a prayer from what you have discovered about your city. For example, my city is Vacaville which literally means cow town. *Vacaville, you are a place of rest, good people, and a crossroads for many streams to flow through. You are the city of peace. You are meant to be a place where revival and refreshing flows out of. Creativity is meant to arise from within you as you love on the King. He'll reveal his secrets to you.* There are so many ways to pray for a city but the main goal is to pray in such a way that your heart starts coming alive for that place.

6. Finally, how deep did your city get into your heart during this exercise? Between 1 to 5, five being you so fell in love with your city and one being I did the exercise but I didn't feel much heart connect for my city. Write your number here and why you wrote that.

Discovering Your Metron as an Emerging Prophet

Day 10: Putting your location discovery together.

Now look through the last 9 weeks of location studies.
Write the name of each nation, state, region, and city you prayed for and list the rating of each location next to the name. Ratings 1-5:

Day	Location	Rating
1	Any nation:	
2	African nation:	
3	Asian nation:	
4	European nation:	
5	South American nation:	
6	Australia/New Zealand/islands:	
7	Your country:	
8	Your state/region:	
9	Your city:	

Which location(s) most captured your heart?

Now continue this journey of greater discovery to see if there are other locations in that part of the world that captures your heart. Go through the prayer journey again. Now with the revelation of what locations are on your heart, what is the next step you should take in moving towards discovering if that location is a place for you to influence or one of many you are called to influence?

Is that location somewhere you should visit? Why and When?

Discovering Your Metron as an Emerging Prophet

If your top pick was a country, can you find the same nationality of people in the country where you live? Does it satisfy your heart to impact that ethnic group in your region or do you feel the need to go to the specific nation of your top pick? Explain.

What ways can you start engaging your heart to explore that nation/location?
(E.g. More Prayer, supporting a Missionary already going there, connecting to people online from there)

Is there a door of influence that is open for you in that country/location?

What is the next step to further the discovery of the places you are called to influence?

Section 2
Discovering The Leaders You Are Called to Impact

    Years ago I started a journal to pray and track the things God was showing me for the leaders I am called to connect with. I would meet different leaders from around the world. Some were in business, others in politics, and others in the entertainment industry. Some were more influential then others but the main thing was I had a connection with them and felt that a significant exchange in the Kingdom could happen. As I prayed for them and put them on my list they got into my heart. I realized that anyone that got into my heart in prayer would eventually get a download from heaven that would be a blessing to them, a prophecy or an encouraging conversation. When it was the right time to give the prophetic word, whether in person, email, phone or Skype, there would be an impact there. Their hearts would be drawn to mine and mine theirs in that interaction. I would then begin to find the ones that I was called to impact.

    In a similar fashion we are going to go on a discovery journey to help you find the leaders you are called to impact. This is a part of your Kingdom platform as a prophet. Nathan the prophet's main role was to impact King David. One King was his main assignment. In ministering to David, Nathan helped set the course of Israel's history and David's history. Over the next 10 journal entries, we will go through a set of prayers to discover who the types of leaders are that you are called to minister to. You may find you land in one particular area that you tend to have more favor in or you may find you have favor amongst a variety of leaders. You may also find that in different seasons your influence shifts to other regions that you presently don't have influence in.

Discovering Your Metron as an Emerging Prophet

Here are the types of leaders you will pray into and discover who you are most passionate to influence.

1. Business/finance leaders
2. Government/political Leaders
3. Media/entertainment/sports/arts leaders
4. Leaders in education/school systems and family
5. Leaders in religions outside of Christianity, e.g. New Age or Mormons

Day 1: Business/Finance Leaders

1. Pray and prophesy over a leader in business today that you know of but don't know personally. Write the prayer and prophecy here. See how much you can prophesy over them without studying up on them.

2. What is their name?

3. Now study up on them. What did you learn about them? What are their strengths, weaknesses, needs, goals, accomplishments, mottos, family dynamics, areas of influence? Now pray and prophesy over them again with that increased knowledge and heart concerning them. Write out the prophecy and prayer here.

4. Between 1-5 how excited did you get to pray into the business arena? One being you're not excited all the way to five being very excited.

Day 2: Business/Finance Leaders

1. Pray and prophesy over a leader in business that you **do know personally or could get to know**. Write out the prophecy and prayer here.

2. What is their name?

3. What is their occupation?

4. Do you have favor with them? What does that look like?

5. Study up on them as much as you are able to. What are their strengths, weaknesses, family dynamics, goals, accomplishments, and anything else that could help give you a bigger heart for them? Now craft another prayer and prophecy with that increased revelation. Write it below. Should you give this word to them or just keep it in your prayer journal?

6. Was it more exciting getting a word for this business leader because you knew them? How excited are you to impact the business arena? One being you're not excited all the way to five being very excited.

Day 3: Politics/Government Leader

1. Pray and prophesy over a leader in politics/government at a local, regional, national, or international level today that you know of but don't know personally. Write the prayer and prophecy here. See how much you can prophesy over them without studying up on them.

2. What is their name?

3. What is their occupation?

Discovering Your Metron as an Emerging Prophet

4. Now study up on them. What did you learn about them? What are their strengths, weaknesses, needs, goals, accomplishments, mottos, family dynamics, areas of influence? Now pray and prophesy over them again with that increased knowledge and heart concerning them. Write out the prophecy and prayer here.

5. Between 1-5 how excited did you get to pray into the political arena? One being you're not excited all the way to five being very excited.

Discovering Your Metron as an Emerging Prophet

Day 4: Politics/Government Leaders

1. Pray and prophesy over a leader in politics/government that you do know personally or could get to know. They could be a local police officer, or the city manager, etc. I used to minister to both of those in the small town I lived in. It is amazing that after you get a heart and an understanding on how to relate to leaders at that level, then God can give you leaders to impact at a much larger level. It doesn't have to be that way for all of us as some of our metrons may have been designed by God to be for a small city rather then a large nation. Either will be fulfilling if you're within the area God has assigned you to. But learning this skill will prepare you for whatever realm of influence he has assigned you to.

So write out a prophecy and prayer here for them.

2. What is their name?

3. What is their occupation?

4. Do you have favor with them? What does that look like?

5. Study up on them as much as you are able to. What are their strengths, weaknesses, family dynamics, goals, accomplishments, and anything else that could help give you a bigger heart for them? Now craft another prayer and prophecy with that increased revelation. Write it below. Should you give this word to them or just keep it in your prayer journal?

6. Was it more exciting getting a word for this political leader because you knew them? How excited are you to impact the political arena? One being you're not excited all the way to five being very excited.

Day 5: Media/Entertainment/Sports/Arts Leaders

1. Pray and prophesy over a leader in this arena today that you know of but don't know personally. Write the prayer and prophecy here. See how much you can prophesy over them without studying up on them.

2. What is their name?

3. Now study up on them. What did you learn about them? What are their strengths, weaknesses, needs, goals, accomplishments, mottos, family dynamics, areas of influence? Now pray and prophesy over them again with that increased knowledge and heart concerning them. Write out the prophecy and prayer here.

4. Between 1-5 how excited did you get to pray into this arena? One being you're not excited all the way to five being very excited.

Day 6: Media/Entertainment/Sports/Arts Leaders

1. Pray and prophesy over a leader in this arena that you do know personally or could get to know. Write out the prophecy and prayer here.

2. What is their name?

3. What is their occupation?

4. Do you have favor with them? What does that look like?

5. Study up on them as much as you are able to. What are their strengths, weaknesses, family, goals, accomplishments, and anything else that could help give you a bigger heart for them? Now craft another prayer and prophecy with that increased revelation. Write it below. Should you give this word to them or just keep it in your prayer journal?

6. Was it more exciting getting a word for this leader because you knew them? How excited are you to impact this arena? One being you're not excited all the way to five being very excited.

Day 7: Education/School Systems and Family Mountain Leaders

1. Pray and prophesy over a leader in this arena today that you know of but don't know personally. Write the prayer and prophecy here. See how much you can prophesy over them without studying up on them.

2. What is their name?

3. What is their occupation?

4. Now study up on them. What did you learn about them? What are their strengths, weaknesses, needs, goals, accomplishments, mottos, family dynamics, areas of influence? Now pray and prophesy over them again with that increased knowledge and heart concerning them. Write out the prophecy and prayer here.

5. Between 1-5 how excited did you get to pray into this arena? One being you're not excited all the way to five being very excited.

Day 8: Education/School Systems and Family Mountain Leaders

1. Pray and prophesy over a leader in this arena that you do know personally or could get to know. Write out the prophecy and prayer here.

2. What is their name?

3. What is their occupation?

4. Do you have favor with them? What does that look like?

5. Study up on them as much as you are able to. What are their strengths, weaknesses, family, goals, accomplishments, and anything else that could help give you a bigger heart for them? Now craft another prayer and prophecy with that increased revelation. Write it below. Should you give this word to them or just keep it in your prayer journal?

6. Was it more exciting getting a word for this leader because you knew them? How excited are you to impact this arena? One being you're not excited all the way to five being very excited.

Day 9: Leaders in Religions outside of Christianity, e.g. New Age or Mormons

1. Pray and prophesy over a leader in this arena today that you know of but don't know personally. Write the prayer and prophecy here. See how much you can prophesy over them without studying up on them.

2. What is their name?

3. What is their occupation?

4. Now study up on them. What did you learn about them? What are their strengths, weaknesses, needs, goals, accomplishments, mottos, family dynamics, areas of influence? Now pray and prophesy over them again with that increased knowledge and heart concerning them. Write out the prophecy and prayer here.

5. Between 1-5 how excited did you get to pray into this arena? One being you're not excited all the way to five being very excited.

Day 10: Leaders in Religions Outside of Christianity, e.g. New Age or Mormons

1. Pray and prophesy over a leader in this arena that you **do know personally or could get to know**. Write out the prophecy and prayer here.

2. What is their name?

3. What is their occupation?

4. Do you have favor with them? What does that look like?

5. Study up on them as much as you are able to. What are their strengths, weaknesses, family, goals, accomplishments, and anything else that could help give you a bigger heart for them? Now craft another prayer and prophecy with that increased revelation. Write it below. Should you give this word to them or just keep it in your prayer journal?

6. Was it more exciting getting a word for this leader because you knew them? How excited are you to impact this arena? One being you're not excited all the way to five being very excited.

Discovering Your Metron as an Emerging Prophet

Final assessment of the last ten days of journaling over the different leaders

Write out the results of your last 10 entries here.

Day	Name of Leader	Level of Excitement
1	Business:	
2	Business:	
3	Political:	
4	Political:	
5	Arts/entertainment/media/sports:	
6	Arts/entertainment/media/sports:	
7	Education/family:	
8	Education/family:	
9	Religious:	
10	Religious:	

What particular area of the 5 areas studied over the last 10 journal entries had the most interest and highest ratings?

What people of influence piqued your interest the most?

Do a deeper discovery of this area and people.

Discovering Your Metron as an Emerging Prophet

What action steps could you take to further build a connection and passion here?

Now do a study for several months just in this area of passion.

Discover if this is a sphere of influence or the main area of influence you're called to.

Section 3
Discovering the Realms of Society You are Called to impact

In this section we are going to do a discovery of the particular realms of society you have a passion for rather then the leaders themselves. Sometimes you can discover your place of influence by the passion you have for a particular arena. Areas that particularly pique your interest that you need to explore. For instance, I've had seasons where I get saturated with passion to study up on the entertainment arena, or to learn about business, or to get immersed into political studies. In those seasons I will find that the more I get an understanding for that realm of society, the easier it is for God to open a door for me in that area. I discover influence always comes to those who are prepared. So I prepare myself through study, prayer, and prophecy. Over the next ten journal entries, we will do a study and prayer journey on the different realms of society. This is different than studying up on the leaders of those societies, although you can include particular leaders in your studies that are relevant to the study of these particular realms. People in these places of influence come and go but the realm itself remains. So we are looking to see if we have a particularly high passion for one or two of these realms of society.

Discovering Your Metron as an Emerging Prophet

Day 1: Business Arena

1. Do a study up on a particular business of interest near your location.

2. What is the business?

3. What did you learn?

4. What is the history of that business?

5. The challenges for that business?

6. As you now take the issues, history, and things you've discovered about that business, begin to pray and prophesy into that business. What do you see in prayer and prophetically for that business?

7. Has your heart been ignited to see that business impacted for the glory of God? Between 1-5, how excited are you to impact the business arena? One being you're not excited all the way to five being very excited.

Day 2: A National Business

1. Do a study up on a particular business of interest in your nation.

2. What is the business? Where is the business located? How many locations does the business have?

3. Do a thorough study of that business. What did you learn?

4. What is the history of that business?

5. The challenges for that business?

6. As you now take the issues, history, and things you've discovered about that business, begin to pray and prophesy into that business. What do you see in prayer and prophetically for that business?

7. Has your heart been ignited to see that business impacted for the glory of God? Between 1-5, how excited are you to impact the business arena? One being you're not excited all the way to five being very excited.

Day 3: Government/Politics

1. Study up on your local city or regional government. What are the strengths, weaknesses, and challenges your local government faces?

2. Who in office do you have a heart for? Why?

3. Pray for them – what did the Lord show you?

4. As you are studying up on your local government, what issues in the local government do you have a heart to see changed?

5. Now prophesy into the situations and issues you want to see changed. What is the Lord's heart for those situations and issues?

6. Has your heart been ignited to see your local government impacted for the glory of God? Between 1-5, how excited are you to impact the local government arena? One being you're not excited all the way to five being very excited.

Day 4: National Government/Politics

1. Study up on your national government. What are the strengths, weaknesses, and challenges your national government faces?

2. Who in office do you have a heart for? Why?

3. Pray for them – what did the Lord show you about them?

4. As you are studying up on your national government what issues in the government do you have a heart to see changed?

5. Now prophesy into the situations and issues you want to see changed. What is the Lord's heart for those situations and issues?

6. Has your heart been ignited to see your national government impacted for the glory of God? Between 1-5, how excited are you to impact the national government arena? One being you're not excited all the way to five being very excited.

Day 5: Sports and Entertainment

1. Study up on one particular actor/athlete of your choice that you have a heart for. What is their name?

2. What are some of their strengths, weaknesses, and history?

3. Why are you drawn to in this actor/athlete? Is it the integrity of their character, the good morals, the bad morals, the lawlessness of their behavior? Why are you drawn to them?

4. Pray and prophesy over them. Write out what you saw.

5. Do you have a heart for particular actors/athletes like this one, many different actors/athletes, or just this particular actor/athlete?

6. Has your heart been ignited to see this actor/athlete and this arena of influence impacted for the glory of God? Between 1-5, how excited are you to impact the entertainment/sports arena? One being you're not excited all the way to five being very excited.

Day 6: Music/Art

1. Study up on one particular leader of your choice in the area of music, or art that you have a heart for. What is their name?

2. What are some of their strengths, weaknesses, and history?

3. Why are you drawn to this leader? Is it the integrity of their character, the good morals, the bad morals, the lawlessness of their behavior? Their leadership? Why are you drawn to them?

4. Pray and prophesy over them. Write out what you saw.

5. Are you drawn to this particular arena as a whole or to the individual influencers within the system? Why are you drawn in that particular direction?

6. Has your heart been ignited to see this leader and this arena of influence impacted for the glory of God? Between 1-5, how excited are you to impact this particular arena? One being you're not excited all the way to five being very excited.

Day 7: Media

1. Study up on one media tycoon or person with inventive ideas for technology. Large or small in influence. E.g. Facebook, Apple.

2. What are their strengths, weaknesses, history, family distinctives, etc.?

3. What and how did they or are they building their media influence?

4. Take some time to pray and prophesy over them and the industry they represent. What do you see for that industry? What is God's heart for that arena?

5. What is the level of influence this person or the kind of technology they have created have on society? Do you have a heart for this specific person or the realm of influence they work within? Why?

6. Has your heart been ignited to see this leader and this arena of influence impacted for the glory of God? Between 1-5, how excited are you to impact this particular arena? One being you're not excited all the way to five being very excited.

Day 8: The Education Arena

1. What school systems grab your heart the most? (E.g. College, high school, junior high, private schools, elementary schools, etc.) Why?

2. Pick one arena that particularly grabs your attention. Now pick a particular school within that arena. (E.g. If you live in San Francisco, pick a high school in San Francisco that you live near that would be easy to pray into.) What are the strengths and weaknesses of that particular school?

3. What is the history of that school? What are the issues that school faces?

4. Now pray and prophesy over that particular school until you get God's heart for it. What did he show you?

5. Has your heart been ignited to see this arena of influence impacted for the glory of God? Between 1-5, how excited are you to impact this particular arena? One being you're not excited all the way to five being very excited.

Day 9: Family Arena

1. What family issues most capture your heart's attention? (Ex. Divorce, foster kids, dysfunctional families, homosexuality, anger, identity crisis, abuse, etc.)

2. What values are you most passionate to see established in the family culture around you? (E.g. Healthy marriages, healthy families, great parenting, forgiveness, reconciliation between different people groups, etc.)

3. Pray into one particular issue in this arena you would like to see changed for the better? What did God show you? What do you think the problem is? What is the solution?

4. What groups are perpetuating the entrenchment of this particular wrong family value? Why do you think they are doing this?

5. Now prophesy God's heart into these issues and the people entrenched in the issues. What is he showing you?

6. Has your heart been ignited to see this this arena of influence impacted for the glory of God? Between 1-5, how excited are you to impact this particular arena? One being you're not excited all the way to five being you're very excited.

Day 10: Religion

1. What religion do you most want to see impacted with Christ? (Catholicism, new age, Muslims, Hindu's, Mormonism, Wicca, etc.) Why?

2. What are the issues of that religion? What is that religion's history?

3. Find some pictures of the people in that religion. Study up on their songs, strongholds, weaknesses, and strengths. What did you discover? What are success stories of those in history who impacted this particular religion for Christ?

4. Now pray for this particular group of people. What are some of the strategies God is showing you to impact them? What are any prophetic words you get for them?

5. Do you know any particular individuals in this religion? Pray for them and ask God to give you a prophetic word and a strategy to reach them. Write it below.

6. Has your heart been ignited to see this this arena of influence impacted for the glory of God? Between 1-5, how excited are you to impact this particular arena? One being you're not excited all the way to five being you're very excited

Discovering Your Metron as an Emerging Prophet

Assessment of the last ten days of journaling over each area of influence

1. Write out the names of the people, companies, etc. you prayed for and the level of excitement you experienced to impact and pray for them between 1-5.

Day	Name of People, Companies, etc.	Level of Excitement
1	Local business:	
2	National business:	
3	Local government	
4	National government:	
5	Entertainment/sports:	
6	Arts/music:	
7	Media:	
8	Education:	
9	Family:	
10	Religion:	

2. After doing this exercise, what specific areas do you feel most passionate for?

3. What specific people do you feel most passionate for?

4. Which leaders most easily brought excitement to your heart to pray for and consider connecting and partnering with?

5. What particular issues within these realms of society do you feel most passionate to explore in order to impact at a higher level?

6. What did you learn about yourself and your God given passions in this particular discovery?

7. Now flush out this study farther by taking the top picks from this series of prayer times and further pray into those you felt the most excitement for. See if your heart for them leads to a relationship with them or a way to impact them.

Section 4
Discovering The People Groups You Are Called to Influence

    I've gone through several years of praying for nations and at the end of that time, my heart was burning with passion for so many nations. My prayer was give me the nations. All I wanted to do was travel to the nations. Then I got invited to speak to the youth in our local church. I didn't want to do that. I wanted to impact the nations. But God sometimes wants to take us on some other journeys of discovery beyond our understanding. He has another arena for us to impact beyond what we understand. So I reluctantly decided to speak to the youth. During the preparation time, I said "God I can't speak to them without your heart." I prayed for his heart for them. As I got ready to speak to them, I began to realize they needed fathers. I said "God give them fathers; give them those that carry your heart for them." Little did I know I was about to be the answer to my own prayer. That night I spoke to the youth. During that message I got a heart for them. They were crying and I was crying. God was supernaturally impacting both of our hearts. It wasn't but a couple weeks later that my leaders asked me to oversee the youth. At first I couldn't figure it out. I had been praying for the nations. But now I'm being offered the youth. God wanted to spend some time developing in me a sustainable love for the next generation. I worked with the youth for three years. Now wherever I go in the world I see youth. I love youth. I want to see them impacted for his glory. The influence I have for youth came out of my heart of prayer for them and then the years of leading them as their youth pastor.

    We are going to take the next 10 journal entries to discover the people groups that God may want us to connect to at a higher level. Prayer is the way to lead us there and help us discover what is in our hearts. Jesus told his disciples in Matthew 9 to pray for the Lord of the harvest to send workers. Then in chapter 10 you see him sending them out. Once we pray and get his heart for someone and something, then God actually empowers us to be a part of the answer to who we were praying to see impacted. He's kind of sneaky like that. Ha Ha. Jehovah Sneaky. But he is good and I've discovered every one of those journeys has always ended up so fulfilling.

    In this particular journey we're not going to pray over every type of people group out there. Study and pray up on the ones that are included in this workbook. You may have a particular people group that is your passion but is not included in the study. I'd encourage you to glean from the heart of this journal discovery time in prayer for other groups but then add your particular group as part of the last discovery entry in this journal.

Discovering Your Metron as an Emerging Prophet

Discovering Your Metron as an Emerging Prophet

Day 1: Youth

1. Do you already have a big heart for youth between 12-18 years of age? Why? How did you get it? If not no worries. Let's go on a discovery to see if this is an area of passion you are called to.

2. Who do you know around you that is a youth? What is their name? What are their strengths, weaknesses, and challenges?

3. What issues are the youth of our day facing?

4. What strengths do you see in the youth of this day?

5. Pray for and get a prophetic word for the youth as a whole and the particular youth you know that you wrote down in the above discovery question.

6. Has your heart been ignited to see youth impacted for the glory of God? Between 1-5, how excited are you to see youth impacted? One being you're not excited all the way to five being you're very excited.

Day 2: Children

1. Do you already have a big heart for children between 0-11 years old? Why? How did you get it? If not no worries. Let's go on a discovery to see if this is an area of passion you are called to.

2. Who do you know around you that is a child? What is their name? What are their strengths, weaknesses, and challenges?

3. What issues are the children of our day facing?

4. What strengths do you see in the children of this day?

5. Pray for and get a prophetic word for the children as a whole and the particular children you personally know that you wrote down in the above discovery question.

6. Has your heart been ignited to see children impacted for the glory of God? Between 1-5, how excited are you to see children impacted? One being you're not excited all the way to five being you're very excited.

Day 3: Elderly

1. Do you already have a big heart for the elderly between 60-100 years old? Why? How did you get it? If not no worries. Let's go on a discovery to see if this is an area of passion you are called to.

2. Who do you know around you that is elderly? What is their name? What are their strengths, weaknesses, and challenges?

3. What issues are the elderly of our day facing?

4. What strengths do you see in the elderly of this day?

5. Pray for and get a prophetic word for the elderly as a whole and the particular elderly you know that you wrote down in the above discovery question.

6. Has your heart been ignited to see the elderly impacted for the glory of God? Between 1-5, how excited are you to see the elderly impacted? One being you're not excited all the way to five being you're very excited.

Day 4: Young adults

1. Do you already have a big heart for young adults between 18-30 years of age? Why? How did you get it? If not no worries. Let's go on a discovery to see if this is an area of passion you are called to.

2. Who do you know around you that is a young adult? What is their name? What are their strengths, weaknesses, and challenges?

3. What issues are the young adults of our day facing?

4. What strengths do you see in the young adults of this day?

5. Pray for and get a prophetic word for the young adults as a whole and the particular young adult you know that you wrote down in the above discovery question.

6. Has your heart been ignited to see young adults impacted for the glory of God? Between 1-5, how excited are you to see young adults impacted? One being you're not excited all the way to five being you're very excited.

Day 5: Middle Aged

1. Do you already have a big heart for the middle aged between 30-60 years old? Why? How did you get it? If not no worries. Let's go on a discovery to see if this is an area of passion you are called to.

2. Who do you know around you that is middle aged? What is their name? What are their strengths, weaknesses, and challenges?

3. What issues are the middle aged of our day facing?

Discovering Your Metron as an Emerging Prophet

4. What strengths do you see in the middle aged of this day?

5. Pray for and get a prophetic word for the middle aged as a whole and the particular middle aged you know that you wrote down in the above discovery question.

6. Has your heart been ignited to see the middle aged impacted for the glory of God? Between 1-5, how excited are you to see the middle aged impacted? One being you're not excited all the way to five being you're very excited.

Day 6: Single adults

1. Do you already have a big heart for adults that are single? Why? How did you get it? If not no worries. Let's go on a discovery to see if this is an area of passion you are called to.

2. Who do you know around you that is single? What is their name? What are their strengths, weaknesses, and challenges?

3. What issues do single adults of our day face?

4. What strengths do you see in the single adults of this day?

5. Pray for and get a prophetic word for the single adults of our day as a whole and the particular single adult you know that you wrote down in the above discovery question.

6. Has your heart been ignited to see single adults impacted for the glory of God? Between 1-5, how excited are you to see single adults impacted? One being you're not excited all the way to five being you're very excited.

Day 7: Marriages

1. Do you already have a big heart for married couples? Why? How did you get it? If not no worries. Let's go on a discovery to see if this is an area of passion you are called to.

2. What one particular couple around you do you know that is married that you'd like to pray for? What are their names? What are their strengths, weaknesses, and challenges?

3. What issues are married couples of our day facing?

4. What strengths do you see in those that are married in today's world?

5. Pray for and get a prophetic word for those that are married as a whole and the particular married couple you know that you wrote down in the above discovery question.

6. Has your heart been ignited to see married couples and marriages impacted for the glory of God? Between 1-5, how excited are you to see marriages impacted? One being you're not excited all the way to five being you're very excited.

Day 8: Poor

1. Do you already have a big heart for the poor? Why? How did you get it? If not no worries. Let's go on a discovery to see if this is an area of passion you are called to.

2. Who do you know around you that is a poor? What is their name? What are their strengths, weaknesses, and challenges?

3. What issues are the poor of our day facing?

4. What strengths do you see in the poor of this day?

5. Pray for and get a prophetic word for the poor as a whole and a particular poor person or community you know.

6. Has your heart been ignited to see the poor impacted for the glory of God? Between 1-5, how excited are you to see the poor impacted? One being you're not excited all the way to five being you're very excited.

Day 9: Wealthy

1. Do you already have a big heart for the financially wealthy? Why? How did you get it? If not no worries. Let's go on a discovery to see if this is an area of passion you are called to.

2. Who do you know around you that is wealthy? What is their name? What are their strengths, weaknesses, and challenges?

3. What issues are the wealthy of our day facing?

4. What strengths do you see in the wealthy of this day?

5. Pray for and get a prophetic word for the wealthy as a whole and a particular wealthy person you know that you wrote down in the above discovery question.

6. Has your heart been ignited to see the wealthy impacted for the glory of God? Between 1-5, how excited are you to see the wealthy impacted? One being you're not excited all the way to five being you're very excited.

Discovering Your Metron as an Emerging Prophet

Day 10: Assessment of the last nine days of journaling over different people groups you want to see impacted.

1. Write out the particular names you prayed for in the particular groups as well as the level of excitement you had in your heart for them between 1-5.

Day	Name You Prayed for	Level of Excitement
1	Youth:	
2	Children:	
3	Elderly:	
4	Young Adults:	
5	Middle Aged:	
6	Single:	
7	Married couples:	
8	Poor:	
9	Wealthy:	

2. After doing this exercise what specific area of people do you feel most passionate for?

3. What specific issues do you feel most passionate to bring change in?

4. Which people group most easily brought excitement to your heart to pray for and consider connecting and partnering with?

5. Which type of person do you know God has called you to pray for but it's not always easy?

6. What did you learn about yourself and your God given passions in this particular discovery?

7. Now flush out this study farther by taking the top picks from this series of prayer times and further pray into those you felt the most excitement for. See if the heart for them leads to a relationship with them or a way to impact them.

Section 5
Discovering The Issues You Are Called to Deal With

King Saul was anointed to be King but it wasn't until a particular group in Israel got messed with by an enemy that he stepped into his calling as King. I Samuel 11:5, "Just then Saul was returning from the fields, behind his oxen, and he asked, 'What is wrong with the people? Why are they weeping?' Then they repeated to him what the men of Jabesh had said. When Saul heard their words, the Spirit of God came upon him in power, and he burned with anger." Sometimes it takes a particular injustice in the areas we are called to impact to arouse us from our normal life to step into the place of impact and the platform of influence in the sphere of influence we are called to step onto. God makes us a prophetic voice to bring change. People bring change through a variety of ways. People like Reese Howells brought change through prayer in the day when Adolf Hitler was taking country after country and destroying them. Others have brought change through action, leadership, and petitions. People like William Wilberforce brought change to the slave laws in his day. Now it's our turn to bring a change, our own unique way.

The Kingdom is only going to be taken by people consumed with passion for heaven to come and the devil's kingdom to be destroyed. In this workbook section, we will discover what are the areas that get us passionate. We will also discover what are the areas that get us upset, and consumed with passion and zeal. Scripture says in **Isaiah 9:7,** "Of the increase of his government and peace there will be no end... The zeal of the LORD Almighty will accomplish this." The zeal of the Lord is the passion of God inside of us that gets released when injustice raises its head in our midst or in the people around us. It is like the passion that I get when I see immorality continually permeating society through the media mountain in California. I am moved to bring a change and my heart begins to burn in prayer, preaching, and influence to change it.

Now in this workbook discovery process, every area of injustice in our hearts we know is wrong. No passionate for God Christian believer would agree with an injustice or want to see it survive. But there are some issues that we are personally called to deal with. We may be grieved with every area of injustice but some areas of injustice like with Saul we will be provoked to action. Those are the areas we are after discovering. We are not saying if we do not have a high passion to see one area changed that we have a bad heart, we are merely trying to find the injustices we are called by God to bring change in. So let's find out what you're passionate about changing.

Discovering Your Metron as an Emerging Prophet

Discovering Your Metron as an Emerging Prophet

Day 1: Racism

1. How does this issue affect you? Between 1-5 right now what is the passion level within you as you hear about this issue? One being it doesn't regularly bother you or five being you get regularly upset or passionate about it.

2. Why does this issue regularly bother or not bother you?

3. Study up on this issue. Do you see this issue running rampant in your area? Nation? Where? Why is it running rampant?

4. What do you think the answer is to deal with this issue? Pray for a few minutes and get God's heart for those under the injustice of this issue.

5. After studying up on this issue do you feel your heart has changed towards this issue of injustice? Between 1 to 5, one being your heart is concerned about this area but won't make a major ministry out of it to five you would give your time energy and life to see this issue changed.

Discovering Your Metron as an Emerging Prophet

Day 2: Impurity

1. How does this issue affect you? Between 1-5 right now what is the passion level within you as you hear about this issue? One being it doesn't continually bother you or five being you get regularly upset or passionate about it.

2. Why does this issue regularly bother or not bother you?

3. Study up on this issue. Do you see this issue running rampant in your area? Nation? Where? Why is it running rampant?

4. What do you think the answer is to deal with this issue? Pray for a few minutes and get God's heart for those under the injustice of this issue.

5. After studying up on this issue do you feel your heart has changed towards this issue of injustice? Between 1 to 5, one being your heart is concerned about this area but won't make a major ministry out of it to five you would give your time energy and life to see this issue changed.

Day 3: Sex Trafficking

1. How does this issue affect you? Between 1-5 right now what is the passion level within you as you hear about this issue? One being it doesn't regularly bother you or five being you regularly get upset or passionate about it.

2. Why does this issue regularly bother or not bother you?

3. Study up on this issue. Do you see this issue running rampant in your area? Nation? Where? Why is it running rampant?

4. What do you think the answer is to deal with this issue? Pray for a few minutes and get God's heart for those under the injustice of this issue.

5. After studying up on this issue do you feel your heart has changed towards this issue of injustice? Between 1 to 5, one being your heart is concerned about this area but won't make a major ministry out of it to five you would give your time energy and life to see this issue changed.

Day 4: Abused Women

1. How does this issue affect you? Between 1-5 right now what is the passion level within you as you hear about this issue? One being it doesn't regularly bother you or five being you regularly get upset or passionate about it.

2. Why does this issue regularly bother or not bother you?

3. Study up on this issue. Do you see this issue running rampant in your area? Nation? Where? Why is it running rampant?

4. What do you think the answer is to deal with this issue? Pray for a few minutes and get God's heart for those under the injustice of this issue.

5. After studying up on this issue do you feel your heart has changed towards this issue of injustice? Between 1 to 5, one being your heart is concerned about this area but won't make a major ministry out of it to five you would give your time energy and life to see this issue changed.

Day 5: Abortion

1. How does this issue affect you? Between 1-5 right now what is the passion level within you as you hear about this issue? One being it doesn't regularly bother you or five being you regularly get upset or passionate about it.

2. Why does this issue regularly bother or not bother you?

3. Study up on this issue. Do you see this issue running rampant in your area? Nation? Where? Why is it running rampant?

4. What do you think the answer is to deal with this issue? Pray for a few minutes and get God's heart for those under the injustice of this issue.

5. After studying up on this issue do you feel your heart has changed towards this issue of injustice? Between 1 to 5, one being your heart is concerned about this area but won't make a major ministry out of it to five you would give your time energy and life to see this issue changed.

Discovering Your Metron as an Emerging Prophet

Day 6: War/Murder/holocaust

1. How does this issue affect you? Between 1-5 right now what is the passion level within you as you hear about this issue? One being it doesn't regularly bother you or five being you regularly get upset or passionate about it.

2. Why does this issue regularly bother or not bother you?

3. Study up on this issue. Do you see this issue running rampant in your area? Nation? Where? Why is it running rampant?

4. What do you think the answer is to deal with this issue? Pray for a few minutes and get God's heart for those under the injustice of this issue.

5. After studying up on this issue do you feel your heart has changed towards this issue of injustice? Between 1 to 5, one being your heart is concerned about this area but won't make a major ministry out of it to five you would give your time energy and life to see this issue changed.

Day 7: Missing or abducted Children

1. How does this issue affect you? Between 1-5 right now what is the passion level within you as you hear about this issue? One being it doesn't regularly bother you or five being you regularly get upset or passionate about it.

2. Why does this issue regularly bother or not bother you?

3. Study up on this issue. Do you see this issue running rampant in your area? Nation? Where? Why is it running rampant?

Discovering Your Metron as an Emerging Prophet

4. What do you think the answer is to deal with this issue? Pray for a few minutes and get God's heart for those under the injustice of this issue.

5. After studying up on this issue do you feel your heart has changed towards this issue of injustice? Between 1 to 5, one being your heart is concerned about this area but won't make a major ministry out of it to five you would give your time energy and life to see this issue changed.

Discovering Your Metron as an Emerging Prophet

Day 8: Corruption in Government or Business

1. How does this issue affect you? Between 1-5 right now what is the passion level within you as you hear about this issue? One being it doesn't regularly bother you or five being you regularly get upset or passionate about it.

2. Why does this issue regularly bother or not bother you?

3. Study up on this issue. Do you see this issue running rampant in your area? Nation? Where? Why is it running rampant?

4. What do you think the answer is to deal with this issue? Pray for a few minutes and get God's heart for those under the injustice of this issue.

5. After studying up on this issue do you feel your heart has changed towards this issue of injustice? Between 1 to 5, one being your heart is concerned about this area but won't make a major ministry out of it to five you would give your time energy and life to see this issue changed.

Discovering Your Metron as an Emerging Prophet

Day 9: Choose an injustice issue that you personally get affected by and study and pray into it today.

1. What is the issue? How does this issue affect you? Between 1-5 right now what is the passion level within you as you hear about this issue? One being it doesn't regularly bother you or five being you regularly get upset or passionate about it.

2. Why does this issue regularly bother or not bother you?

3. Study up on this issue. Do you see this issue running rampant in your area? Nation? Where? Why is it running rampant?

4. What do you think the answer is to deal with this issue? Pray for a few minutes and get God's heart for those under the injustice of this issue.

5. After studying up on this issue do you feel your heart has changed towards this issue of injustice? Between 1 to 5, one being your heart is concerned about this area but won't make a major ministry out of it to five you would give your time energy and life to see this issue changed.

Discovering Your Metron as an Emerging Prophet

Day 10: Assessment of the last nine days of journaling over issues of injustice

Day	Issue	Level of Excitement
1	Racism	
2	Impurity	
3	Sex Trafficking	
4	Abused Women	
5	Abortion	
6	War/murder/holocaust	
7	Missing or abducted children	
8	Corruption in Government or Business	
9	Injustice of your choice:	

2. After doing this exercise what specific areas do you feel most passionate for?

3. What specific people do you feel most passionate to help?

4. Have you already taken steps towards ministering to those in the areas you were most passionate to see changed?

5. What steps should you take to begin to discover further if you are called into reaching the people under this injustice?

6. What could you do to change this issue?

7. Have you received any prophetic words about the areas you are most passionate to see changed?

8. Now flush out this study farther by taking the top picks from this series of prayer times and further pray into those that you felt the most burden for. See if your heart for them leads to a prophetic ministry in this area or a way to impact those being influenced by this injustice.

Section 6
Discovering the Kingdom Leaders You're Called To

Years ago I started a systematic approach to connecting to Kingdom leaders. When you pray for a leader you get a heart for them, this often results in you getting an assignment for or with them. I've seen this happen many times in my life. Before I get a role to influence leaders and even partner with them, I have to get a heart for them. Recently I kept seeing a leader from another church movement. I had a heart for him and every time I saw him a prophetic word started bubbling up in my heart for him. After about the third time randomly seeing him in a city I came up to him and gave him the word. It really impacted his life and the next thing I knew I was being invited to pray and prophesy over the leaders of his network. I'm not saying this is a formula but I've noticed this trend working quite often in my life. First I get a heart for someone and then a door opens to impact or partner with him or her. These are different then the previous leaders we studied up on. These leaders are believers. They may be leaders in the gathered church context or the scattered church context. They could be leaders in the vocational ministry or leaders in the marketplace ministry. Whatever arena they are in the goal is to discover God's heart for them through prayer. We will spend time asking the Lord to give us a prophetic word for them. Prayer opens doors of favor and the prophetic word gives influence. God can cause us to connect to leaders in many ways besides this. But this is one approach that I have found helpful in discovering his heart for leaders.

As I said, I've spent years systematically putting on a list the names of pastors, prophets, and Kingdom leaders from different streams, churches, and areas of society. I made it a habit to pray for them and at certain times I methodically called, emailed or texted many of them with no other agenda than to just love on them. I didn't connect with them to get a connection or a meeting or an open door, I connected to them for their sake. God decides who the doors of influence should be opened to and when someone should invite me into their world. But getting his heart for different leaders gives him something to work with and where your compassion is you will soon see miracles. The compassion God has given me as I have prayed for these leaders opens their hearts to being impacted and allows heaven to influence them in a way that brings life to their world. What a joy it is to partner with heaven in this. So let's discover who you're called to impact.

Discovering Your Metron as an Emerging Prophet

Day 1: Pray for a local pastor

1. What is the name of a local pastor you'd like to pray for?

2. What is their specific role as a pastor?

3. How many people do they impact?

4. What are the needs you perceive in prayer?

5. What is their family like?

6. What is God's heart for them? Pray over them and all those they are called to pastor until you begin to get God's heart of compassion for the load they carry.

7. Begin to stir up your heart for them until a prophetic word begins to come forth for them. Write it down below.

8. How easy was it to get a heart for this pastor? No need to feel guilty if your level of excitement isn't that high to impact this leader. This may be showing you an arena you will or won't have a high impact in. Between 1-5, what is the level of heart connect and excitement to impact this leader. Write down one being you're not excited all the way to five being very excited.

Discovering Your Metron as an Emerging Prophet

Day 2: Pray for an apostle you know of or are familiar with

1. What is the name of the Apostle you'd like to pray for?

2. What is their specific role as an apostle?

3. How many people do they impact?

4. What are the needs you perceive in prayer?

5. What is their family like?

6. What is God's heart for them? Pray over them and all those they are called to be an apostle to until you begin to get God's heart of compassion for the load they carry.

7. Begin to stir up your heart for them until a prophetic word begins to come forth for them. Write it down below.

8. How easy was it to get a heart for this apostle? No need to feel guilty if your level of excitement isn't that high to impact this leader. This may be showing you an arena you will or won't have a high impact in. Between 1-5, what is the level of heart connect and excitement to impact this leader. Write down one being you're not excited all the way to five being very excited to impact them.

Discovering Your Metron as an Emerging Prophet

Day 3: Pray for a prophet you know of or are familiar with

1. What is the name of the prophet you'd like to pray for?

2. What is their specific role as a prophet?

3. How many people do they impact?

4. What are the needs you perceive in prayer?

5. What is their family like?

6. What is God's heart for them? Pray over them and all those they are called to be a prophet to until you begin to get God's heart of compassion for the load they carry.

7. Begin to stir up your heart for them until a prophetic word begins to come forth for them. Write it down below.

8. How easy was it to get a heart for this prophet? No need to feel guilty if your level of excitement isn't that high to impact this leader. This may be showing you an arena you will or won't have a high impact in. Between 1-5, what is the level of heart connect and excitement to impact this leader. Write down one being you're not excited all the way to five being very excited.

Discovering Your Metron as an Emerging Prophet

Day 4: Pray for a specific pastor in your local church
(E.g., youth pastor, children's pastor, worship pastor.)

1. What is the name of the pastor you'd like to pray for?

2. What is their specific role as a pastor?

3. How many people do they impact?

4. What are the needs you perceive in prayer?

5. What is their family like?

6. What is God's heart for them? Pray over them and all those they are called to pastor until you begin to get God's heart of compassion for the load they carry.

7. Begin to stir up your heart for them until a prophetic word begins to come forth for them. Write it down below.

8. How easy was it to get a heart for this pastor? No need to feel guilty if your level of excitement isn't that high to impact this leader. This may be showing you an arena you will or won't have a high impact in. Between 1-5, what is the level of heart connect and excitement to impact this leader. Write down one being you're not excited all the way to five being very excited.

Discovering Your Metron as an Emerging Prophet

Day 5: Pray for a specialty ministry leader outside the local church
   (E.g., Prison ministry, Gideon's ministry, homeless ministry, etc.)

1. What is the name of the leader you'd like to pray for?

2. What is their specific role in their ministry?

3. How many people do they impact?

4. What are the needs you perceive in prayer?

5. What is their family like?

6. What is God's heart for them? Pray over them and all those they are called to minister to until you begin to get God's heart of compassion for the load they carry.

7. Begin to stir up your heart for them until a prophetic word begins to come forth for them. Write it down below.

8. How easy was it to get a heart for this leader? No need to feel guilty if your level of excitement isn't that high to impact this leader. This may be showing you an arena you will or won't have a high impact in. Between 1-5, what is the level of heart connect and excitement to impact this leader. Write down one being you're not excited all the way to five being very excited.

Discovering Your Metron as an Emerging Prophet

Day 6: Pray for an outreach or evangelist minister

1. What is the name of the outreach/evangelist minister you'd like to pray for?

2. What is their specific role and what do they do in this ministry?

3. How many people do they impact?

4. What are the needs you perceive in prayer?

5. What is their family like?

6. What is God's heart for them? Pray over them and all those they are called to reach until you begin to get God's heart of compassion for the load they carry.

7. Begin to stir up your heart for them until a prophetic word begins to come forth for them. Write it down below.

8. How easy was it to get a heart for this evangelist/outreach leader? No need to feel guilty if your level of excitement isn't that high to impact this leader. This may be showing you an arena you will or won't have a high impact in. Between 1-5, what is the level of heart connect and excitement to impact this leader. Write down one being you're not excited all the way to five being very excited.

Day 7: Pray for a kingdom teacher

1. What is the name of the teacher you'd like to pray for?

2. What is their specific role and area to train in as a teacher?

3. How many people do they impact?

4. What are the needs you perceive in prayer?

5. What is their family like?

6. What is God's heart for them? Pray over them and all those they are called to teach until you begin to get God's heart of compassion for the load they carry.

7. Begin to stir up your heart for them until a prophetic word begins to come forth for them. Write it down below.

8. How easy was it to get a heart for this teacher? No need to feel guilty if your level of excitement isn't that high to impact this leader. This may be showing you an arena you will or won't have a high impact in. Between 1-5, what is the level of heart connect and excitement to impact this leader. Write down one being you're not excited all the way to five being very excited.

Day 8: Pray for an international ministry leader

1. What is the name of the international ministry leader you'd like to pray for?

2. What is their specific role as a leader?

3. How many people do they impact?

4. What are the needs you perceive in prayer?

5. What is their family like?

6. What is God's heart for them? Pray over them and all those they are called to lead until you begin to get God's heart of compassion for the load they carry.

Discovering Your Metron as an Emerging Prophet

7. Begin to stir up your heart for them until a prophetic word begins to come forth for them. Write it down below.

8. How easy was it to get a heart for this leader? No need to feel guilty if your level of excitement isn't that high to impact this leader. This may be showing you an arena you will or won't have a high impact in. Between 1-5, what is the level of heart connect and excitement to impact this leader. Write down one being you're not excited all the way to five being very excited.

Discovering Your Metron as an Emerging Prophet

Day 9: Pray for someone who has a ministry into one of the spheres of society

1. What is the name of the leader you'd like to pray for?

2. What is their specific role of ministry in society?

3. How many people do they impact?

4. What are the needs you perceive in prayer?

5. What is their family like?

6. What is God's heart for them? Pray over them and all those they are called to impact until you begin to get God's heart of compassion for the load they carry.

7. Begin to stir up your heart for them until a prophetic word begins to come forth for them. Write it down below.

8. How easy was it to get a heart for this leader? No need to feel guilty if your level of excitement isn't that high to impact this leader. This may be showing you an arena you will or won't have a high impact in. Between 1-5, what is the level of heart connect and excitement to impact this leader. Write down one being you're not excited all the way to five being very excited.

Discovering Your Metron as an Emerging Prophet

Day 10: Assessment day of the last nine days of journaling over Kingdom leaders

1. Write out the leaders names you prayed for and the level of excitement you had to pray for each of them between 1-5.

Day	Leader's Name	Level of Excitement
1		
2		
3		
4		
5		
6		
7		
8		
9		
10		

2. After doing this exercise, what specific areas do you feel most passionate for?

3. What specific people do you feel most passionate for?

4. Which leader most easily brought excitement to your heart to pray for and consider connecting and partnering with?

Discovering Your Metron as an Emerging Prophet

5. Which type of leader do you know God has called you to pray for but it's not always easy?

6. Which leader do you most resonate with?

7. What did you learn about yourself and your God given passions in this particular discovery?

8. Now flush out this study farther by taking the top picks from this series of prayer times and further pray into those you felt the most excitement for. See if the heart for them leads to a relationship with them or a way to impact them.

Discovering Your Metron as an Emerging Prophet

Final Assessment Summary of all you've discovered in this journal:

Now you are going to assimilate the answers with the highest passion scores from each of the 6 sections in the journal you have spent the last 3 months going through. Write out the top two answers and ratings for each category.

Section	Description	Top Score	2nd Top Score
1	Discovering the places you're called to influence		
2	Discovering the leaders you're called to influence		
3	Discovering the realms of society you're called to impact		
4	Discovering the people groups you are called to influence		
5	Discovering the issues you are called to deal with		
6	Discovering the kingdom leaders you're called To		

Fill in the blanks below according to the answers you entered above.

Section 1. I am called to influence the

Section 2. I am called to influence these kind of leaders

Section 3. I have a passion for these realms of society

Section 4. I am called to help change these particular people groups

Section 5. I am called to deal with these kinds of issues

Section 6 I am called to partner with these kinds of business leaders

Now look at each of the categories.

Can you see any commonalities between the different areas you scored highest in?

What should be your next step after flushing out this discovery journal?

Who should you begin to pray about connecting with?

What countries should you pray about visiting?

What locations should you pray about going to?

What arenas of influence should you explore further to see how your influence flushes out there?

Discovering Your Metron as an Emerging Prophet

What should be your next step in dealing with the injustices that were the highest on your list?

How can you move forward in developing partnerships with the Kingdom leaders you scored the highest with?

Discovering Your Metron as an Emerging Prophet

Create an action plan and then begin your journey towards your platform as an emerging prophet.

God Bless you!
Keith Ferrante

ABOUT THE AUTHOR

Keith Ferrante is a 3rd generation pastor who travels internationally speaking in churches, conferences, ministry schools and other venues. Keith carries a message of reformation with the core foundations of joy, freedom and family. He is a prophetic voice who carries a breaker anointing to open up the heavens and bringing timely corporate words. Keith carries the heart of the Father and has a passion to equip the body of Christ for the work of the ministry with kingdom influence, in and outside of the church meeting context. Keith also does Kingdom consulting for leaders in the business world, church world and other areas of influence.

Keith and his wife, Heather, serve on the leadership team of The Mission, in Vacaville, CA. Prior to that, they spent ten years as Senior Leaders at Shiloh Gateway of Worship in Willits, California. They have shown a consistent lifestyle of walking out what they teach and impart. Over the past 15 years they have overseen, planted and worked with a variety of ministry schools in the United States and internationally. They carry an anointing to break heavens open over churches, regions and nations through presence based ministry, prophetic teaching and impartation. They have traveled to many nations bringing people into radical encounters with God. People experience joy, freedom, deliverance, healing and the love of God in their meetings.

To contact Keith and Heather to schedule a ministry event, prophetic consultation, or host a prophet school in your area go to: **www.emergingprophets.com**

Made in the USA
Columbia, SC
12 February 2023

12036690R10087